Buzzing Bee

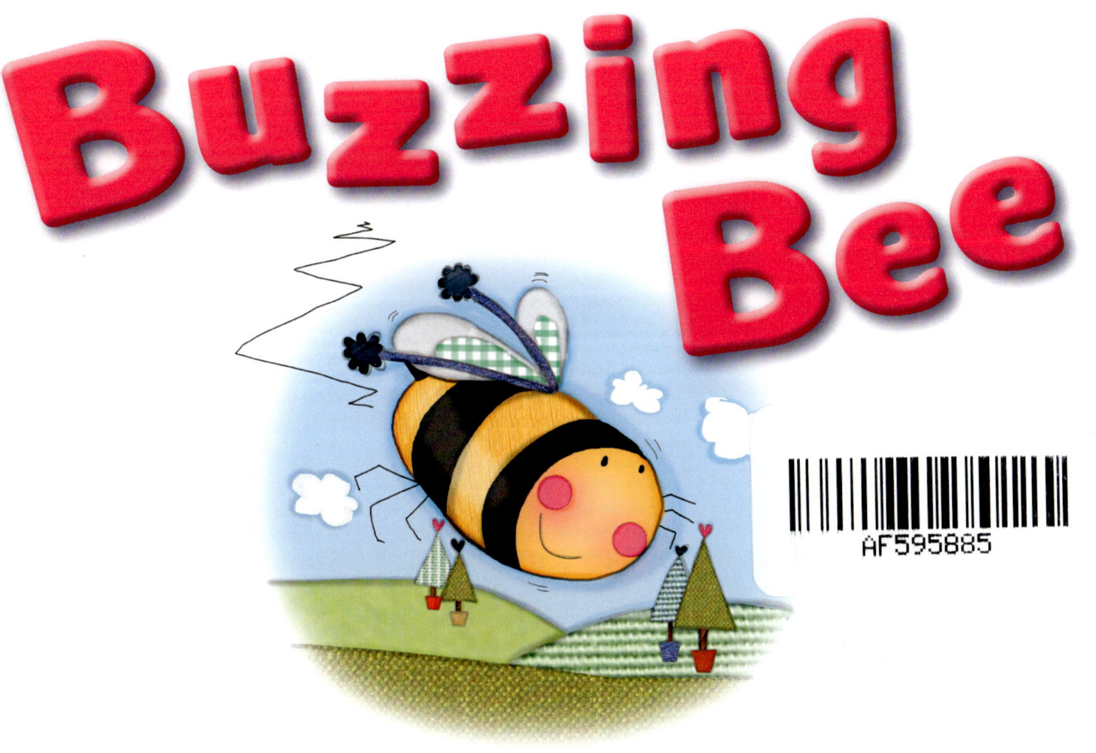

Monica Hughes

Illustrated by Katie Saunders

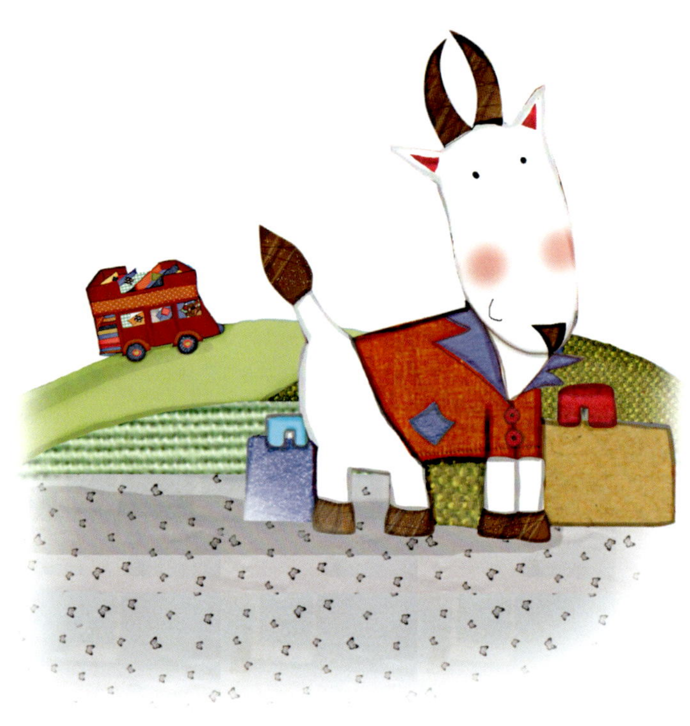

a goat in a coat

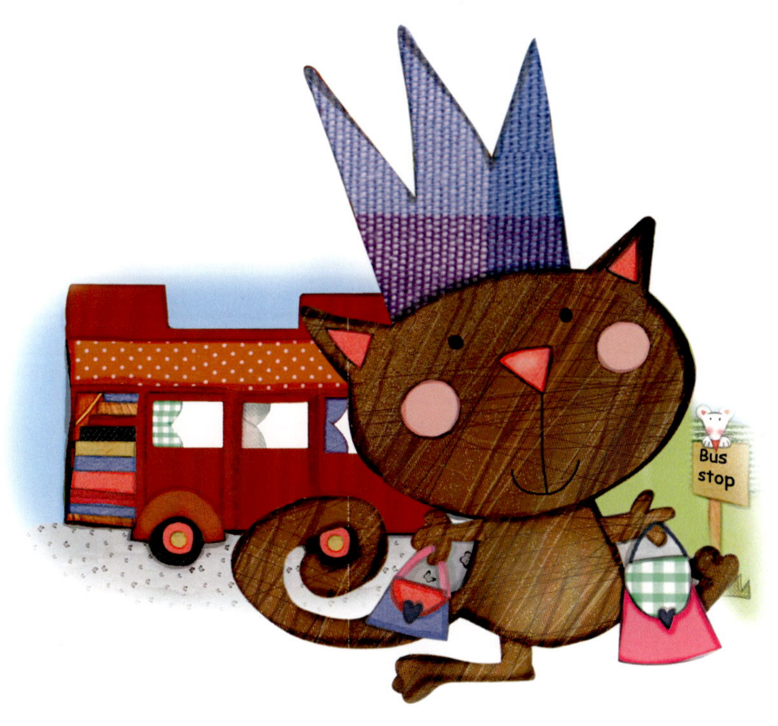

a cat in a hat

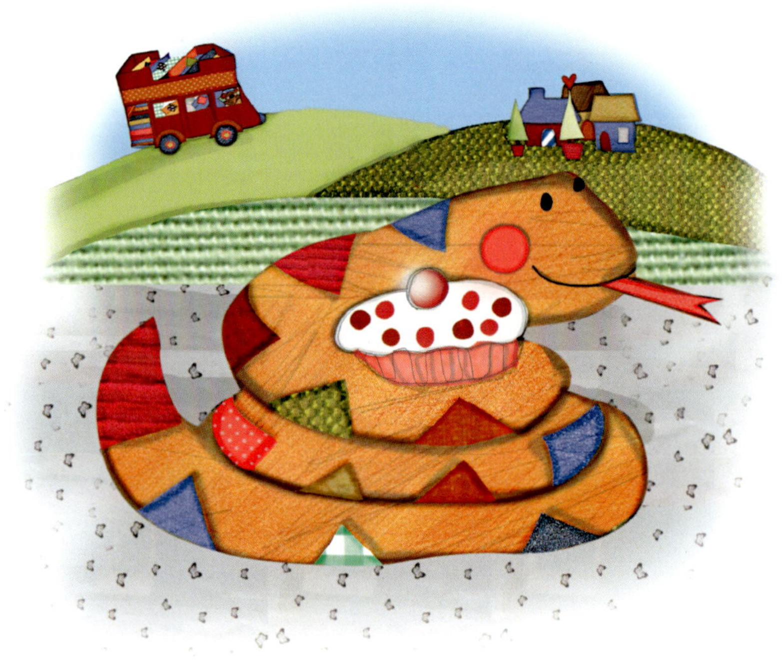

a snake with a cake

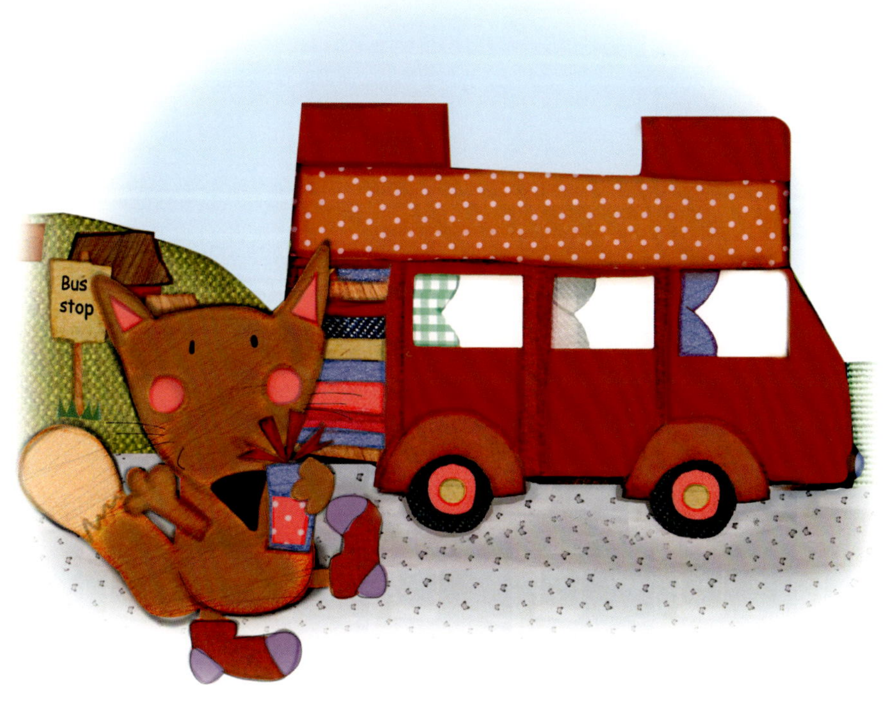

a fox with a box

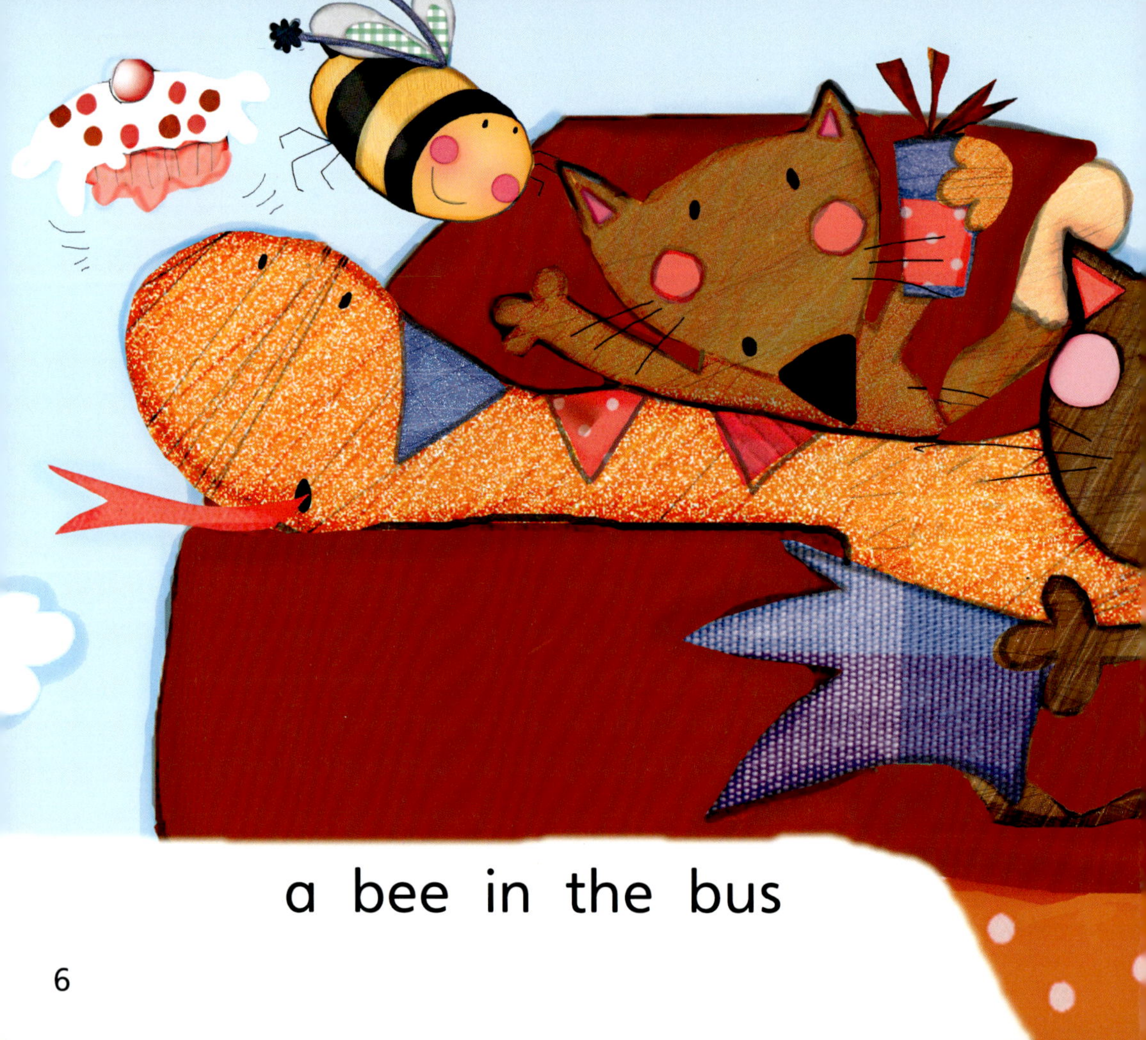

a bee in the bus

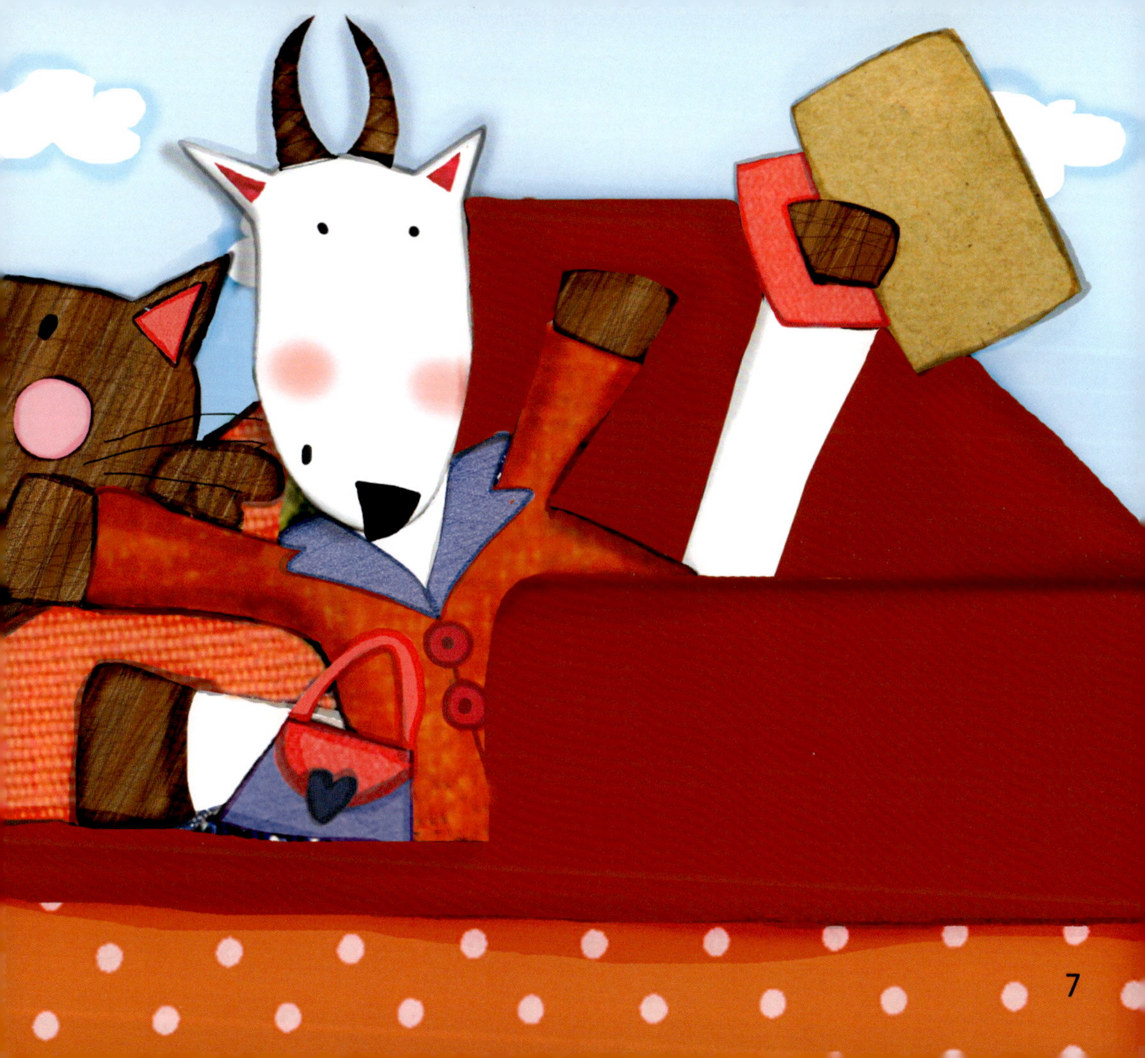

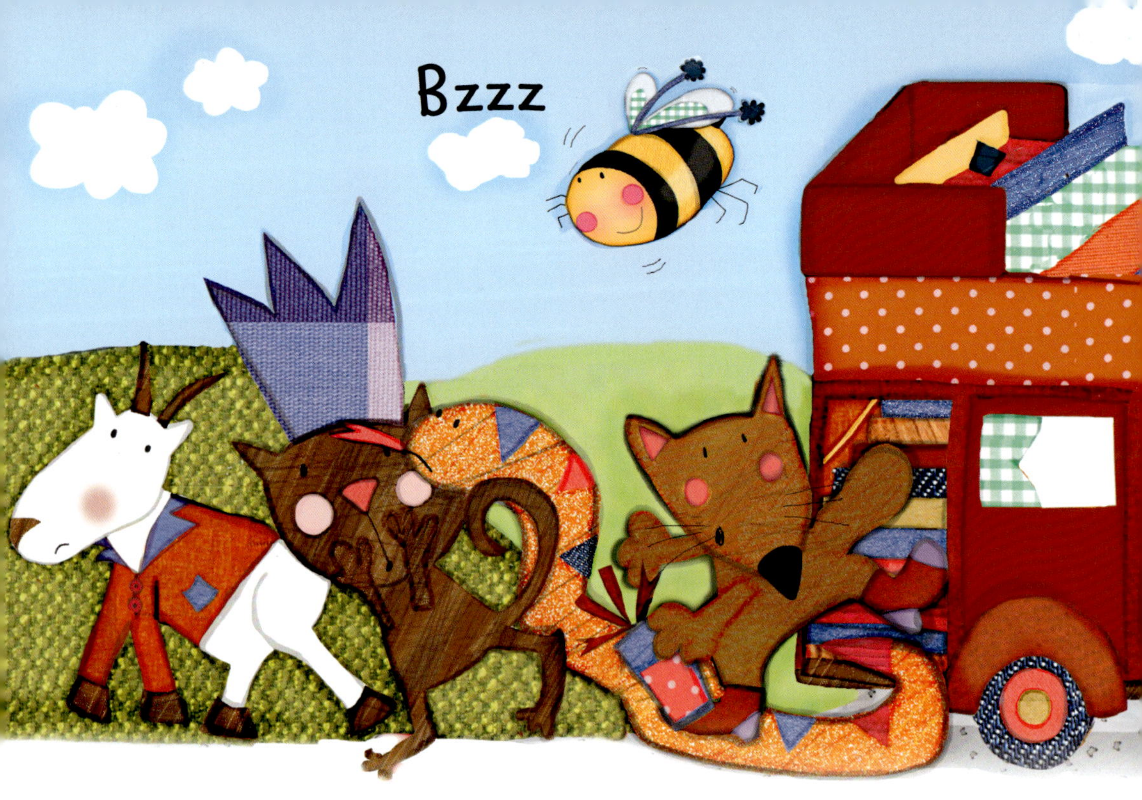

Bzzz Bzzz Bzzz